To

From

Date

Quiet Moments
in the Garden

Kay Arthur
Emilie Barnes
Julie Clinton
Elizabeth George
Sharon Jaynes
Stormie Omartian
Jennifer Rothschild
Lysa TerKeurst

Artwork by
Annie LePoint

HARVEST HOUSE PUBLISHERS

EUGENE, OREGON

Harvest House Publishers has made every effort to trace the ownership of all poems and quotes. In the event of a question arising from the use of a poem or quote, we regret any error made and will be pleased to make the necessary correction in future editions of this book.

Cover and interior design by Garborg Design Works, Savage, Minnesota.

Artwork © Annie LaPoint, Licensed by Penny Lane Publishing, Inc.

QUIET MOMENTS IN THE GARDEN
Copyright © 2011 by Harvest House Publishers
Published by Harvest House Publishers
Eugene, Oregon 97402
www.harvesthousepublishers.com
ISBN 978-0-7369-3852-5
Portions of the text were taken from *Walking with God in the Quiet Places.*

Printed in China

11 12 13 14 15 16 17 18 / FC / 10 9 8 7 6 5 4 3 2 1

> *To cultivate a garden is to walk with God.*
>
> CHRISTIAN NEVELL BOVEE

> *But as for me, how good it is to be near God!*
> *I have made the Sovereign LORD my shelter,*
> *and I will tell everyone about the wonderful things you do.*
>
> PSALM 73:28 NLT

ELIZABETH GEORGE

Counting on God's Grace and Peace

Grace to you and peace be multiplied.

1 PETER 1:2 NKJV

You're a special woman. I know it. Do you know how I know? You're pursuing grace and peace by spending time in these devotions and in God's Word. When God lives within us, His Spirit causes us to yearn for a gentle calm in our lives.

Are you struggling or suffering? Are you facing a painful loss? A common response women have when they're first asked to contemplate a gentle and quiet spirit is to declare, "But I can't be like that. I can't remain calm when there's trouble." True…if we're relying on our own strength. But when we appropriate God's great enablers—His grace and His peace—we can achieve gentleness and calmness even during hard times. We just need to…

- *count on God's grace.* It's given. It's here. It's available.

- *pray for God's grace.* Your awareness of God's grace will expand when you give more things and more of you to Him.

- *get on with life.* Regardless of our struggles, it's possible—and important—to have something positive to show for our suffering, including how much God loves us, cares for us, and provides for us.

From God's Word to Your Heart

It's wonderful to think about God's grace and peace. They are two of the loveliest gifts He bestows on us. The very words move our souls.

Grace is active and means "favor." So whatever your situation, whatever the occasion, you have God's favor. You have what you need to endure, cope, and have victory. Peter prays that God's grace will be with the people he's writing to…including you and me.

Peace, on the other hand, is passive and refers to rest. And so, dear one, whatever your situation, whatever the occasion or need, you have God's peace. You have God's rest *in* your suffering.

Yes, as we suffer for doing what's right and are enabled by the power

of God's grace and enjoying His peace, as we put on
God's gentle and quiet spirit and rely on the Lord instead of
our human efforts and emotions, as we wait on Him to help
us make sense of our suffering times, then indeed we
have much to show in the end. Every time we endure
hard times, we prove that the glory of the Lord
is truly revealed in the end. As the psalmist
declared, "Oh, taste and see that the LORD
is good; blessed is the man [or woman] who
trusts in Him!" (Psalm 34:8 NKJV).

*God, I cry out to You during this
time of strife. Your grace and
peace lead me to
adopt a gentle and
quiet spirit even
now…especially
now. I will trust in
Your strength
and not my
own as I
wait for Your
healing and
direction.
Amen.*

You are my hiding place; you will protect me from trouble and surround me with songs of deliverance.

PSALM 32:7 NIV

See! The winter is past; the rains are over and gone. Flowers appear on the earth; the season of singing has come, the cooing of doves is heard in our land.

SONG OF SOLOMON 2:11 NIV

7

EMILIE BARNES

A Treasure in Jars of Clay

But we have this treasure in jars of clay to show that
this all-surpassing power is from God and not from us.

2 CORINTHIANS 4:7 NIV

When our son, Brad, was in high school, he really enjoyed taking courses in ceramics. Even though I am his mother, I can say he was very good. In fact, many of his prized vases, jars, and pots still adorn our home. When I looked at a lump of reddish-tan clay, I was amazed that Brad was able to make a beautiful vessel out of it. When he added color and glaze, it became a masterpiece.

In today's scripture we read that we are "jars of clay." We have a great treasure in us, and this all-surpassing power is from God and not from us.

We live in a world that tells us that if we are righteous enough we can become little gods. However, our reading says that we (Christians) are jars of clay with this great treasure (Jesus Christ) in us. I can go to any nursery in our area and purchase an inexpensive clay pot. They're not of much value. On the other hand, my dictionary defines "treasure" as wealth or riches, something of great value. While we hide our treasures in vaults or safe-deposit boxes, God trusts His treasure in a common clay pot! The only value our clay pot has is in the treasure inside.

If we believe that this is true, then we will want to share that treasure inside of us with others. I am continually amazed how God can use me, just an ordinary person. We need to show others

that this all-surpassing power is from God and not from us. Philippians 4:13 (NIV) states, "I can do everything through him who gives me strength."

Can you trust God today to believe that you, a clay pot with a great treasure inside, can do all things because Christ Jesus has given you the strength and power to do it? If we could believe this promise, we would change ourselves, our families, our churches, our cities, our country, and the world. Trust God today for this belief.

Father God, even though I am an inexpensive clay pot, You make me valuable because You live in me. Thank You for that gift. Amen.

Where flowers bloom so does hope.

LADY BIRD JOHNSON

9

Julie Clinton

The Trust Fall

*Trust in him at all times, O people; pour out your hearts to him,
for God is our refuge.*

PSALM 62:8 NIV

Trusting God to reveal His dream in your life and give you hope often requires an extraordinary act of willpower. It's kind of like one of those "trust falls," where you fall backward into the arms of someone you trust to catch you. You give up total control and place absolute trust in that person to catch you in that moment.

God wants to teach you the same about Him—that you're not in control. He is. He wants to show you that when He seems most absent and you're falling backward, He really is most present and there to catch you. God walks beside you even when you can't see, hear, or feel Him. He provides you with what you need to get through deep pain, unbelievable circumstances, and surreal events. In your weakness, He wants you to fall backward, into His arms. Place your trust in Him and let Him prove to you that He will not disappoint.

Nature is the art of God.

DANTE ALIGHIERI

We do not see nature with our eyes, but with our understandings and our hearts.

WILLIAM HAZLITT

Kay Arthur

Words of Faith When Pressures Build

Come to Me, all who are weary and heavy-laden, and I will give you rest.

Matthew 11:28 NASB

Are you living life in overdrive? Do you ever feel like running away, checking out, giving up?

Life is filled with pressure, pressure, pressure.

Pressure to be. Pressure to do. Pressure to perform. Pressure to produce.

And with the pressures come anxiety and stress, especially to the Christian who longs to be pleasing to God.

Am I being the mate I should be? The parent I should be? Am I handling everything the way I ought to as His child?

Life is so accelerated. Hurrying to work. Dashing to get the kids to their activities. Hurrying to prepare meals. Rushing to get to church.

You think you're going to slow down when the kids get back to school…come winter…come Christmas…come summer…come vacation.

But it doesn't happen. Realistically, life is never going to slow down; the pressure is never going to lessen; the stress will always be there in one form or another. So what are you going to do about it? Tough it out until you break? Run into some ungodly escape hatch? Give up? Check out?

The good news is, you don't have to choose any of the above. God knows about the pressure, the stress, the anxiety, the accelerated pace of our earthly life, and He has provided a "way of

13

escape…so that you will be able to endure it" (1 Corinthians 10:13 NASB).

It's all wrapped up in our communion with God, what I call "going into the sanctuary." And there is one element of communion with God that I believe is a vital key to releasing pressure or stress. That key is worship through music: praising God in song.

During Paul's second missionary journey, the apostle and his compatriot Silas found their ministry causing a riot, and they felt the brunt of it. Their clothes were torn from them, and they were beaten and thrown into prison.

Stress? Yes!

Anxiety? Every legitimate reason for it!

How did Paul and Silas handle it? What kept them from breaking?

Acts 16:25 (NASB) gives us the answer: "But about midnight Paul and Silas were praying and singing hymns of praise to God." They turned their focus from the present pressures of their lives to the throne of their sovereign Abba Father—and the tension was relieved.

When sheep become tense, edgy, and restless, the shepherd will quietly move through the flock, and his very presence will release the tension of the sheep and quiet their anxieties. Their shepherd is there!

And this is what happens when we begin to worship our Lord and our God in song. We move into a consciousness of His presence, and the tension begins to unravel, the tautness of the pressure eases, anxieties be-come meaningless, for we are reminded that He is there—our Jehovah Shammah, our all-sufficient, sovereign God. He in-habits the praises of His people (Psalm 22:3).

The more you enter into His courts with praise and into His gates with thanksgiving, the less you will feel the stress, the pressure, the anxiety of daily life, for you will have…

set your mind on the things above, not on the things that are on earth. For you have died and your life is hidden with Christ in God (Colossians 3:2-3 NASB).

True silence is the rest of the mind; it is to the spirit what sleep is to the body, nourishment and refreshment.

WILLIAM PENN

15

Stormie Martian

Refusing to Be Afraid of the Dark

Who walks in darkness and has no light?
Let him trust in the name of the LORD and rely upon his God.

ISAIAH 50:10 NKJV

When I gave birth to my first baby, the doctor told me, "You have a boy." I didn't forget that information and have to keep asking him over and over "What was my baby?" I did not wake up in the hospital the next morning and say to the nurse, "Tell me again what I had." The minute I heard I had a son, no one had to tell me again. From that moment, I knew. An entire vision for my child's future was in place the second I was told the truth.

This experience is the same for every mother and every father. Or anyone who receives life-changing good news. God wants you to have that same certainty about Him. He wants you to be so convinced of His presence in your life that even when you can't feel it, sense it, or see it, you know He is there. He wants you to be completely sure that the light of His Spirit in you will never be put out. You don't have to keep looking for it. You don't have to doubt it. No circumstance can dim it. It is there for now and all eternity.

One of the ways God makes us certain of His light is by allowing us to test it in the darkness. But this darkness is not to be dreaded. It is the darkness God has created for His purposes. "I form the light and create darkness" (Isaiah 45:7 NIV). God sometimes allows things to get very dark in our lives in order to grow us up and teach us about Himself. And some things that we accomplish in darkness cannot happen in any other setting.

Think about what it's like when the power goes out in your home at night. You can barely function in the dark. You walk carefully, one step at a time, reaching out for familiar things to steady and guide you until you can find a flashlight, candle, or generator switch. If someone is holding a source of light, you reach out and take their hand so you can move together. You don't take a step until you're certain that both of you are going in the same direction.

That's exactly how God uses darkness in our lives. We're in the dark until we see *His* light in it. He wants us to reach out for *Him* so we can walk together in the same direction. He desires that we draw close so that we sense His presence at all times.

Prayer Light

Lord, thank You that because I walk with You I don't have to fear the dark. Even in the blackest night, You are there. In the darkest times, You have treasures for me. No matter what I am going through, Your presence and grace are my comfort and my light. Your Word says, "If one walks in the night, he stumbles, because the light is not in him" (John 11:10 NKJV). But I know Your light is in me. I believe in You and know that You have lifted me out of the darkness of hopelessness, futility, and fear. I refuse to be afraid. I give my hand to You, Lord. Take hold of it and lead me. Thank You that as I take each step, the light You give me will be all I need.

$\mathscr{S}$HARON $\mathscr{J}$AYNES

A Child's Faith

A little child will lead them.

Isaiah 11:6 niv

~~~

And dear God," my little boy whispered, "I pray that you give Mommy and Daddy another Jaynes baby."

After four years of praying for God to bless us with a second child, we realized that might not be His plan for our family. However, every night my little boy, Steven, prayed for another "Jaynes baby." But how do you tell someone to stop praying a prayer?

As I pondered this dilemma, God took care of it for me. Just before his fifth birthday, Steven and I were sitting at his child-sized table eating peanut butter and jelly sandwiches. He looked up at me, and with all the wisdom of the prophets, he asked, "Mommy, have you ever thought that God might want you to have only *one* Jaynes baby?"

"Yes, son, I have," I said. "And if that's the case, I'm glad He gave me everything I ever wanted in one package when He gave me you."

"Well, what I think we ought to do is to pray until you're too old to have one. Then we'll know that was His answer."

Steven had no idea how old "too old" was. He knew Sarah in the Bible was 90 when she delivered Isaac. But whatever the outcome,

Steven wasn't having a problem with God saying no. My son knew I said no to him many times, and no didn't mean "I don't love you." Rather it meant "I'm your parent, and I know what's best for you."

God taught me a great lesson that day. Through Steven's childlike faith, God gave me an example of the attitude of trust I should have toward my heavenly Father who loves me and knows what's best for me...and sometimes that means accepting when His answer is no.

More things are wrought by prayer than this world dreams of.

ALFRED LORD TENNYSON

take delight in the Lord, and He will give you the desires of your heart. *Psalm 37:4*

ꞲENNIFER ꞂOTHSCHILD

Burnout or Rest?

*He said to them, "Come with me by yourselves
to a quiet place and get some rest."*

MARK 6:31 NIV

Ꞁ've tried to learn what causes burnout before I smell the smoke! In the past, by the time I detected the burnout, it was like an incinerator, and I was lost in its flames. I'm finally figuring out that rest must be a discipline, and sometimes discipline is hard!

Hebrews 3:19 (NIV) says, "So we see that [the children of Israel] were not able to enter [God's rest], because of their unbelief." God has shown me that when I can't rest (or when I'm flat-out unwilling to), I'm actually unwilling to fully trust in Him.

And that, my friend, sounds a lot like unbelief.

My burnout episodes in past days found their roots in the warped, really silly belief that I had to somehow help God accomplish His will. If I didn't strive, I foolishly reasoned, well, the almighty, omnipotent Lord of the universe wouldn't be successful.

Helping God run the universe is a lofty responsibility and a tough business. It can make a girl tired! Obviously, He can handle it Himself just fine. He doesn't need our assistance; He desires our obedience. Jesus tells us, "Take my yoke upon you and learn from me, for I am gentle and humble in heart, and you will find rest for your souls" (Matthew 11:29 NIV).

I remember reading something Chuck Swindoll wrote years ago that went like this: "The

zealot declares, 'I'd rather *burn* out than *rust* out.' But really, what's the difference? Either way you're out!"

I can't really think of a place in Scripture where God calls us to burn ourselves to a crisp in His service. In fact, He calls us to rest. He calls us to discipline our souls to find rest in Him, not in our accomplishments on His behalf.

Would you drive your car if the gas tank were empty? Of course not. But how often do you keep on driving yourself even when *you* are empty? Benjamin Franklin once said, "He that can take rest is greater than he that can take cities."

Do you know why he compares the ability to rest with world domination? Because both require discipline. We must discipline ourselves to rest—emotionally, mentally, and physically. (And remember, Jennifer is preaching to herself here!)

To really rest means we submit our control to God's calendar, surrender our plans to His direction, and yield our time to His schedule. Even God made time in His busy creation project to rest! So for you to do the same is to follow His example. Disciplining yourself to rest is an act of good stewardship.

The discipline of rest brings freedom that doesn't exist in the ashes of burnout. When we allow ourselves to burn out, we are rendered ineffective to all the goals and tasks that were once our priorities. To discipline ourselves to rest now is far easier than to dig ourselves out of a fire pit later.

God commanded the ancient Israelites to observe the Sabbath every seven days. And He even instructed them to give their land a rest every seven years. My friend, if the dirt needs a rest so it can continue to be fruitful, so do you!

For each new morning with its light,

For rest and shelter of the night,

For health and food, for love and friends,

For everything Thy goodness sends.

RALPH WALDO EMERSON

Lysa TerKeurst

Don't Send Me to Africa

The eyes of the LORD range throughout the earth to strengthen those whose hearts are fully committed to him.

2 CHRONICLES 16:9 NIV

Since I was a little girl I've had a heart for the people of Africa. To be honest, though, I didn't want to be a missionary who lived in a hut, ate grubs fried on an open flame, and wore tribal headdresses. What a limited view of Africa I had. So while I prayed for the people of Africa, I would always throw in, "But, Lord, don't send me." I can just imagine God smiling and looking back at me saying, "Really, princess? You don't want to go to Africa…fine. Then I'll send Africa to you."

And that's exactly what He did. One night while attending a concert by the Liberian Boys Choir, God clearly spoke to my heart and told me that two of those boys were mine. I tried to ignore Him but to no avail. At the end of the concert, two of the boys walked straight up to me, wrapped their arms around me, and called me Mom. After months of prayer and piles of paperwork, we went to pick up our two sons, Mark and Jackson. Africa had come to our home.

No longer was the plight of the starving orphans in Africa a nameless face on TV; they were precious children who deserved a second chance. Not only did we think so, but other people in my church soon felt moved to also adopt children from Liberia. Today, as I walk up to church on Sunday mornings, I am always moved by the precious sight I see. A little white hand holding a little black hand, a brother and sister skipping and laughing together! And something in my heart just knows this is the way it's supposed to be.

This is the way the body of Christ is supposed to work. God speaks, we listen; He confirms, we obey; He gives us the strength to do amazing things, we watch miracles come out of our lives. I love 2 Chronicles 16:9 because it brings a picture to my mind of God standing in front of a crowd of people asking, "Who is willing to do an amazing assignment for Me?"

Many shrug and make excuses. But one little girl jumps up and in complete abandon says, "Me, Lord! Me! Pick me! I am willing!" Then God smiles, scoops her up, brings her into His loving embrace, and whispers back, "Well done, My child. I am so pleased. You have made the good choice. I will give you the strength to do this. Do not be afraid. I will be with you."

Dear Lord, let me always be that little girl with the up-stretched arm and obedient heart. Give me the wisdom to know Your voice and the courage to say yes to whatever You ask of me. My greatest desire is to walk with You all the days of my life. I don't want to settle for the good life. I want the great life, where I live the adventure You created my soul to live. In Jesus' name. Amen.

Julie Clinton

The Hands of Jesus

Be kind and compassionate to one another.

Ephesians 4:32 NIV

Have you ever had a colleague offer a tissue in response to your tears? A neighbor you've never met bring dinner over when she learns your mother passed away? A friend offer to keep your young children so you can fly out to your grandma's funeral? They might not all be Christians, but they are Jesus' hands and feet in dark hours.

All too often, we're uncomfortable letting anyone know that all is not right in our world. We don't want to owe anyone, so we hesitate to accept the help that comes in response to tough times.

But Jesus reaches down from heaven through other people's hands. When we refuse their help, we may actually be refusing Him. We cry out for God's help, but when it comes in the form of another human, we are loath to accept it. For some reason we suddenly let pride stand in the way of allowing God to use other people to show us His love and compassion.

If you're in the midst of tough times right now, how can you let others use their hands to be Jesus to you? Can you accept a meal? An offer of transportation? A willingness to run errands? By saying yes, you'll let Jesus comfort you through the people He's placed specifically and purposefully in your life. Allow Him to serve you.

O Lord Jesus, let me see Your face in the concerned expression of a neighbor who brings me a meal. Let me feel Your arms in the arms of others who give me hugs of reassurance. Let my heart be open to receiving Your love through the people You have put in my life. Amen.

Gratitude is the fairest blossom

which springs from the soul.

HENRY WARD BEECHER

STORMIE OMARTIAN

Learning to Walk

You will show me the path of life; in Your presence is fullness of joy;
at Your right hand are pleasures forevermore.

PSALM 16:11 NKJV

When both of my children learned to walk, they didn't get very far without fall-ing. They fared much better if they reached up and took my hand. Or their father's hand. We were able to guide them away from danger and get them safely where they needed to go. But sometimes they quickly headed off without our help. My son would end up falling down and hurting himself, or my daughter would wander off to someplace she wasn't supposed to go and get into trouble. Occasionally we *allowed* those things to happen because we wanted them to eventually learn to walk *without* our assistance. Of course, we did step in and protect them when we saw danger. But our goal was always to prepare them for the day when they would no longer need our help. And we were thrilled when we saw them experience that joy of freedom for the first time.

Learning to walk with our heavenly Father is somewhat different. He wants us to reach up and take His hand, but He doesn't want us to *ever* let go. In fact, His desire is that we become *more* and *more* dependent upon Him for every step. That's because He wants to take us to places we've never been. To heights we can't even imagine. In order to do that, we have to go through the low valleys, treacherous mountains, rough terrain, and narrow paths of life—places where we could easily get

lost or off the track. And there is definitely no way we can just head off on our own and expect to arrive safely in the place He has planned for us. And, quite opposite of the way we teach our children, we will *never* know the joy of *true* freedom until we understand we cannot take a single step without His help.

But it's up to us to take the first step. We must look into the face of God, reach up to take His hand, and say, "Lead me in the path You have for me, Lord. From this day on I want to walk with You. I take this step of faith and I trust You to meet me here. Align my heart with Yours."

Once you've taken that first step, God will show you other steps to take. He will teach you how to walk in the light of His truth, revelation, and love.

Prayer Light

Father God, I don't want to take one step without You. I reach up for Your hand and ask that You lead me in Your way. Thank You that no matter where I am right now, even if I have gotten way off course, in this moment as I put my hand in Yours, You will make a path from where I am to where I need to be. And You will lead me on it. I love that Your grace abounds to me in that way. And though I can't see exactly where I am going, I'm certain that You can and will enable me to get to where I need to be. Thank You, Lord, that You are teaching me how to walk in total dependence upon You, for I know therein lies my greatest blessing.

ELIZABETH GEORGE

Defining True Wisdom

The wisdom that is from above is first pure, then peaceable, gentle, willing to yield,
full of mercy and good fruits, without partiality and without hypocrisy.
Now the fruit of righteousness is sown in peace by those who make peace.

JAMES 3:17-18 NKJV

A life of lovely graciousness models the fruit of wisdom and its rare fragrances of humility and gentleness. We can tell a lot about a person's faith life by how well she sows wisdom and peace. The world judges beauty by external elements: the style of a woman's hair, the designer labels on her clothes, the monetary value of her house and car. But God's beauty pours forth in the form of edifying godly words of wisdom that bring blessings to its hearers.

Consider these definitions and explanations of the eight components James shares on spiritual wisdom, the kind that comes down from above.

- *Pure*—True wisdom is free from ulterior motives and self-interest.

- *Peaceable*—True wisdom accomplishes peace in our relationships with others and with God.

- *Gentle*—True wisdom offers forgiveness and extends kindness and consideration to everyone.

There is no greatness where
there is not simplicity.

LEO TOLSTOY

Nature is an unlimited broadcasting station, through which God speaks to us every hour, if we will only tune in.

GEORGE WASHINGTON CARVER

- *Willing to yield*—True wisdom is marked by a willingness to listen and a sense of knowing when to yield.

- *Full of mercy*—True wisdom reaches out to help others.

- *Full of good fruits*—True wisdom bears "good fruits" of action.

- *Without partiality*—True wisdom does not waver or vacillate in indecision or play favorites in dispensing truth and holding to its standard.

- *Without hypocrisy*—True wisdom does not deal in deception, pretension, or selfishness.

From God's Word to Your Heart

How did you do with the checklist? Are these "good fruits" evident in your life? Did you find any of these marks of wisdom missing from your lips and your ways? Think a moment about your relationships and your effect on others. Are you a promoter of peace and righteousness?

May yours be a heart of wisdom! And may your words be filled with God's wisdom. And may your prayer be a humble request to never put yourself or your opinions above the needs of others. Become that sower of peace in your family. Speak words of mercy and be sincere in your forgiveness of others. You'll experience the gracious beauty of a life overflowing with true wisdom—God's wisdom.

God, when I rely on my wisdom and the influences of the world, I end up sowing discontent and jealousy. I don't want to rely on my emotions or the trends of the season. I want my life to bear the fruit of Your wisdom so I bring blessings to others and praise to Your name. Amen.

LYSA TERKEURST

His Banner over Me

When the Holy Spirit controls our lives he will produce
this kind of fruit in us: love, joy, peace, patience, kindness,
goodness, faithfulness, gentleness, and self-control.

GALATIANS 5:22-23 TLB

I had just settled into my seat when I noticed a nice-looking young woman boarding the plane. She was tall and slender with a pleasant smile. Wearing jeans and a casual top, nothing particularly made this girl stand out until she got close enough for me to notice the pageant banner draped across her shoulder. "Miss USA," it read in sparkly letters.

My first thought was, *How cool…a real Miss USA.* Visions of me and my sisters as little girls glued to the television danced through my mind. We would all pick a favorite, root for her the whole pageant through, and giggle and prance about as if we were being crowned.

As others noticed Miss USA's banner, they started asking her questions and congratulating her. The flight attendant even made an announcement that a celebrity passenger had just joined us. As she told everyone about Miss USA, the other passengers clapped and cheered for her. She took it all in stride and even seemed a bit

bashful about the attention. That impressed me more than her title. A gentle, humble spirit in the face of such notoriety is something to be admired.

After all the fuss over Miss USA settled down, I started thinking about the banners we all wear every day. While they may not drape across our chest and be printed in bold letters that sparkle, we all say something about who we are just in our countenance and interactions with others. Galatians 5:22-23 describes for us what our banner should read: love, joy, peace, patience, kindness, goodness, gentleness, faithfulness, and self-control. The Bible calls these the fruit of the Spirit, which means they're evidence to others that we are Christians. While others may not applaud us as celebrities, they will notice the difference it makes to have God's Spirit in us if these fruits characterize our interactions with them.

It's important to understand that exemplifying these fruits is a choice we must make every day. Just as Miss USA must intentionally put on her banner, so must we. We must make the choice moment by moment, interaction by interaction, word by word, step-by-step, day by day. When I let another driver over into my lane in traffic, when I smile and thank the grocery store clerk, when I let someone go ahead of me in the coffeehouse line, when I give a gracious answer to someone being harsh with me, when I hold the door for an elderly person, or when I carry the groceries of an overwhelmed mom to her car, I am intentionally choosing to exemplify Christ.

While the world may never applaud or crown me with glory, I imagine Jesus beaming and maybe even applauding.

> *Dear Lord, may the evidence of my love for You be the banner I put on each day. Not so that I may draw attention to myself, but rather to cause other people to want to know what makes me different. I love You, Jesus, and I want to tell the whole world about You, using words only if necessary. In Jesus' name. Amen.*

EMILIE BARNES

I Am Special

I praise you because I am fearfully and wonderfully made;
your works are wonderful, I know that full well.

PSALM 139:14 NIV

One evening our seven-year-old grandson, Chad, was helping me set the dinner table. Whenever the grandchildren come over, we have a tradition of honoring someone at the table with our red plate that says, "You Are Special Today" (even though it isn't a birthday, anniversary, or other special occasion). It was natural for me to ask Chad, "Who should we honor today with our special plate?"

Chad said, "How about *me*?"

"Yes, Chad, you are special," I replied. "It's your day."

He was so proud as we all sat around the table and said our blessing. Then Chad said, "I think it would be very nice if everyone around the table would tell me why they think I'm special." Bob and I got a chuckle out of that, but we thought it might be a good idea, so we did it. After we were all through, Chad said, "Now I want to tell you why I think I'm special. I'm special because I'm a child of God." Chad was so right on. Psalm 139:13-14 tells us that God knew us before we were born. He knit us together in our mother's womb, and we are wonderfully made.

When I was seven, ten, or even twenty-two, I could not have told anyone why I was special. I didn't even talk, I was so shy. My alcoholic father would go into a rage, swearing and throwing things. I was afraid I'd say the wrong thing, so I didn't talk. My self-image wasn't too good.

But the day came when I read Psalm 139, and my heart came alive with the realization that I, too, am special because I am a child of God. And so are you. We were uniquely made as He knit us together in our mother's womb.

Verse 16 says, "All the days [are] ordained for me." It's not by accident you are reading this devotion today. Perhaps you, too, need to know how very special you are. We have all been given unique qualities, talents, and gifts. And you, my dear one, have been made by God. You are His child. He loves you more than any earthly father could possibly love you. Because He is your heavenly Father, Almighty God, He cares for you even when you don't care for yourself. You are His child even when you feel far from Him. It's never your heavenly Father who moves away from you. It's you who move away from Him.

Today is ordained by God for you to draw near to Him and allow Him to be near to you. Because today is your day, my friend, "You Are Special Today." A child of God, as Chad said.

Father God, thank You for making me so special, with a heart to love You more and more each day. Please today help me to draw near to You and to feel Your presence. Thank You for being my heavenly Father. I know that I'm never alone. You are always with me. Amen.

*K*AY *A*RTHUR

Words of Faith When You're Wondering If God Is Enough

I sought the LORD, *and He answered me,*
and delivered me from all my fears.

PSALM 34:4 NASB

*H*ow are you doing…*really doing?*

I would love to knock on your front door and have you invite me in for a cup of coffee and a chat. But since time and distance keep us from doing that, this book must be the next best thing. If we could just spend some time together, when we got past the "Hi! How are you?" I would want to know "How are you doing…really doing?"

How are you doing on the inside? Are you hurting or feeling like a failure? Are you exhausted, tired of what seems like a rat race through the same old maze of life, day in and day out? Are you fighting a battle with disappointment? Depression? Discouragement? Are you feeling unloved or unlovable?

Are you questioning God, wondering why He has allowed things to be the way they are? Maybe you can't even admit this to others for fear they won't understand. Is there anger in your heart because of excruciating pain or bitter disappointment? Because you have lost someone or because your life has not been a "normal" life? Because you have been rejected, abused, neglected, or unloved?

Any one thing in the creation is sufficient to demonstrate a Providence to a humble and grateful mind.

EPICTETUS

Does the future scare you? Are you wondering about your job? Your health? Cancer? Heart problems? Your children? Are you wondering how you are going to care for your parents? How you are going to provide for your family? What will happen in your old age?

Are you worrying? Anxious because you may lose your job…or because you can't find work? Worried about the kids? About how they will turn out? About what they are being exposed to? What they might get into? Drugs? Immorality? Suicide?

Or maybe all is well, but you want to go deeper with God. You want a greater consistency of devotion to your Lord Jesus Christ. You want your life to be different, less commercial, more centered on your Lord and eternal things. You want your life to have eternal significance; you want to be used by Him more than you have been in the past.

Whatever your situation, wherever you are, the answer is always the same: *God knows your plight, your state. He knows exactly where you are and what you are going through.*

He knows, and He wants to give you a future and a hope.

Jennifer Rothschild

Petals

For you know that it was not with perishable things such as silver or gold that you were redeemed from the empty way of life handed down to you from your forefathers, but with the precious blood of Christ, a lamb without blemish or defect. He was chosen before the creation of the world, but was revealed in these last times for your sake. Through him you believe in God, who raised him from the dead and glorified him, and so your faith and hope are in God.

1 Peter 1:18-21 NIV

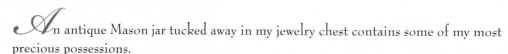

An antique Mason jar tucked away in my jewelry chest contains some of my most precious possessions.

To a casual observer, it may appear that the jar is full of mismatched potpourri. But in reality, each dried flower petal has been placed in the jar quite intentionally over the past 20 years.

Within the antique blue glass are the petals from the first roses that Phil gave me on Valentine's Day when we were dating. Mixed in with these are rose petals from my bridal bouquet, from the roses he gave me on our first wedding anniversary, and from the dozen roses that proudly graced the hospital room after the birth of our first son.

Over the years, more petals have been added. If you look through the hazy glass, you can see miniature buds that once adorned the corsage I wore on Mother's Day after our second son was born. The tiny blossom reminders of my grandmother's funeral are scattered within the

potpourri, along with faded blossoms from roses that my sons presented to me at one of my speaking events.

Though each rose petal is different in color, texture, and size, what they all have in common is that they once complemented beautiful roses, and each represents something very dear to me.

There is another Rose, a precious Rose, that is not contained in my old Mason jar. It is a Rose that first sprang up in ancient Bethlehem. It blossomed in a humble manger, in the garden of poor, ordinary, faithful parents, beneath the pure light of a bright star.

The beauty of the Rose was first beheld by some humble shepherds and later adored by some very wise men. Both humble and high were granted access to the Rose. In the Song of Solomon, many pious Bible students through the years have seen the beauty of Jesus in the one who calls Himself the Rose of Sharon. What a lovely way to communicate who He is to each of us.

The picture of a rose shows Christ's beauty, and it also shows His desirability and accessibility to each of us. The rose is the chief of flowers for its beauty and fragrance, and our Jesus is the preeminent object of our desire. The sweetness of His fragrant life and words adds beauty to our dull and colorless world.

For Christ to be the Rose of Sharon shows that He is the Rose for all. Sharon was the ancient place where roses grew in fields, plentiful and lovely. Jesus was not a rose that sprang up in a greenhouse, reserved for the rich or elite. No, He blossomed in a humble manger, where all could see, touch, and receive Him. His gospel is for all—rich, poor, old, young, seeker, and skeptic.

The Rose of Sharon yields a transcendent perfume that calls us to breathe in His beauty. If you come to the manger to see the Rose, you will notice that it is moistened with dew—the tears of mourning that remind us that He was the Rose destined to wear thorns and to shed the beauty of His scarlet petals for you and for me.

He did, my friend. You are the reason He brought His beauty to this earth. You are the reason; it was for your sin the beautiful Rose was crushed.

You are the reason the Rose arose.

Don't hide the beauty of the Rose of Sharon in a treasure box with all your other sweet memories or keepsakes. Wear the Rose upon your heart, upon your life. So many cynical, despairing people in our unhappy world need to catch the scent of His fragrance and be drawn into His garden.

A thing of beauty is a joy forever.

JOHN KEATS

*God writes the gospel not in the
Bible alone, but on trees and
flowers and clouds and stars.*

Martin Luther

$\mathscr{S}$HARON $\mathscr{J}$AYNES

Your Scars Are Beautiful to God

Let the redeemed of the LORD tell their story.

PSALM 107:2 TNIV

$\mathscr{I}$t was just a few days after Easter, and I was reading about the resurrection of Jesus in the Gospel of John, chapter 20. I had read the story many times before, but this time God revealed something I'd never noticed before.

In my mind's eye I saw Mary weeping in the pre-dawn mist hovering over the garden and the tomb where Jesus' body had been laid three days earlier. I saw her running to tell the disciples of her conversation with the risen Lord. I imagined Peter and John gazing into the empty tomb.

"He's not here," John whispered as he peered inside. "His body is gone."

And later, as the disillusioned band of disciples huddled in their hiding place, I saw Jesus appear in their midst. He didn't knock. He didn't open the door. He simply appeared.

"Peace be with you," Jesus said.

Then I realized that the disciples didn't recognize Him. He looked like Jesus, talked like Jesus, but…how could He be Jesus?

In order to convince them, Jesus made a simple gesture. He held out His arms and revealed His nail-pierced hands.

He lifted up His tunic and uncovered His spear-pierced side.

It was then that they believed.

O God, I prayed, *they didn't recognize Jesus until He showed them His scars.*

Yes, My child, He seemed to say. *This is what I wanted you to see. They didn't recognize Jesus until He showed them His scars, and this is how others still recognize Him today—when men and women who have experienced the healing of past wounds are not ashamed to show their scars to a hurting world.*

In all things of nature there is something of the marvelous.

ARISTOTLE

Never lose an opportunity to see anything that is beautiful, for beauty is God's handwriting—a wayside sacrament. Welcome it in every fair face, every fair sky, every fair flower, and thank God for it as a cup of blessing.

RALPH WALDO EMERSON